For Men, About Women

A Mans Guide to Interpersonal Relationships With Women

by

Cap'n Ron

AuthorHouse™
1663 Liberty Drive
Bloomington, IN 47403
www.authorhouse.com
Phone: 1 (800) 839-8640

Published by AuthorHouse 11/03/2015

ISBN: 978-1-4184-1955-4 (sc)

Library of Congress Control Number: 2004092851

Print information available on the last page.

Any people depicted in stock imagery provided by Thinkstock are
models, and such images are being used for illustrative purposes only.
Certain stock imagery © Thinkstock.

This book is printed on acid-free paper.

Because of the dynamic nature of the Internet, any web
addresses or links contained in this book may have changed
since publication and may no longer be valid. The views
expressed in this work are solely those of the author and do
not necessarily reflect the views of the publisher, and the
publisher hereby disclaims any responsibility for them.

Table of Contents

Introduction

Many times in my life, friends have said to me that I should write a book. I never have figured out just what prompted them to believe I have any literary talents, and up to now, I never really gave it much thought. I never undertook any class in writing, or speech, or anything else involving literature, and the closest I ever came to any culture was eating a bowl of cottage cheese.

This is for men, about women. To bring to light some of the many things that I have learned, by myself, from my own association and encounters with women. Throughout my life, I have heard and have been told many things about what women want, like, don't like, desire, need and hope to find in a man. One of the most often heard issues from women is that their man isn't romantic or sensitive enough, and doesn't take enough time or effort with romancing her. Some women honestly feel that they are nothing more than something a man screws on the bed and then does his laundry and cooks for him.

What I have written is from knowledge I gained from women themselves. The contents herein is a culmination of high points over a period of many years, starting back when I was in the Navy up to now. As a single man in my 50's and who has been married before, I have traveled over many a distance in association with women, and some of the roads weren't paved.

The text is unabridged and to the point, but not vulgar nor obscene. Although I suppose there are those who may view it as such, I offer a thousand celestial apologies in advance. I have never been known to beat around the bush. To coin a well-known phrase, I simply "tell it like it is". As for any women who may be reading this, remember - this written <u>for</u> men, in <u>men's</u> terminology. Men, as a rule, are not politically or grammatically correct, so I didn't write this politically or grammatically correct.

Forewords

"Having known Cap'n Ron for many years and being aware of his creativity, this book is another written treasure of wit. I found many true statements and found myself laughing quite a bit, although I don't particularly care for some of the descriptive words such as 'clam', but it's written for men in the mens' terminology. This book is not for the prudish, but it is ever so true. Kudos for job well done! Cannot wait to see more of his work like this".

-Debbie Kalisz

"A down to earth approach for men in their relationships with women. The text is written in atypical male lingo, and deals with most aspects of romancing women. My husband and I found it to be to the point and with many humorous overtones; although as a woman, I don't agree with some of the statements about women (my husband says I'm in denial). Overall, I believe Cap'n Rons' insight is on the mark and this should be read by adults only, as the text is descriptive but not vulgar".

-Mr. & Mrs. C.J. Bennett

"This being Rons' first attempt at getting something published, I feel it bears comment. I have known him for several years, during which, he has written several articles and short scripts for magazines and newsletters and almost all portray his humorous satire and quick wit in just about ant subject. I can best describe the dude as 'upfront', blatantly honest with often 'flowery' expressions of humor. The straight forward attitude in this book is a refreshing look at male/female relationships. In a day and age where 'reality this' and 'reality that' are the prime buzzwords, this book is about as real as it gets regarding men and women. Definitely a plus reading for guys and should be read with an open mind".

-Wayne Clark

Preface

What I have written is somewhat short, for two reasons: One, most men won't read anything in large volume or thicker than a sports magazine. Also, a man isn't going read something that requires a great deal of time. Two, I am no Guru claiming "infinite wisdom" about women. If I were, I wouldn't be writing this. I'd be holding therapy sessions for men at $500.00 an hour.

The information written herein, is basically to pass on certain things to other men so they can relate in their own personal contact with women. It's something that he can read in the presence of his woman. She shouldn't mind him reading it because what is written in here is to her advantage as well as his. It's better than him flipping through a swimsuit issue, working up a chubby, then wanting her to meet him in the bedroom.

One thing to keep in mind while reading this – this is a generalization, as there is no manual for either men or women, and it is not cast in stone. Everyone is different in their own way and every rule has an exception, but it is through this writing hopefully, that men will become more aware in romancing the female gender. Well, probably not all men, but at least a notable percentage. Throughout life, I have been reminded from time to time that there are but 3 types of men – those who learn by reading, those who learn by observation, and then there's the remainder of those men who just <u>have</u> to pee on the electric fence. This book is basically for the latter. This is not one-sided, as there is no doubt some women will read this as well as men - if for nothing else, out of curiosity.

Having said that, I would like to dedicate this to all the women that I have known, and to all the women of this world. For without them, life for us men would be very mundane to say the least.

Chapter One

Basics

Throughout the ages, men have been in pursuit of women for romance. Not that the women are all that elusive, but they do enjoy being sought after. Men have tried to charm them, impress them, lure them, and then some just went and took them. To this day, the pursuit continues, although the latter mentioned above will get a guy stripes to wear. And the women, to gain the males' attraction, will also resort to luring them, impressing them and charming them. The charming, luring and impressing methods differ between men and women, but none the less they are still used. All for the sake of romance, sex, companionship and comfort.

Men try to be cool, self-decreed "Sultans of Smooth", and the woman is his prey, to be the victim of his suave and debonair ways. Think what you want studly, but you are _her_ subject. She is the one who decides where anything goes.

In any attempts a man may make to romance a woman that turns out successful, he will believe that it is the results of his own efforts. However, the end result is of _her_ choice, _not_ his efforts, because it's the women in the world that are at the controls. As the saying goes, the hand that rocks the cradle rules the world. You may doubt that women call the shots, but they do. They can turn a man's head, lead him on, get him to come to them, cause him to walk into a lamp post, and so on. Face it, all women have to do is smile, bat their eyes

1

and men are toast. Put that with a slight parting of the lips, a longing expression with half closed eyes and we're buttered toast! Some folks may think that doesn't apply anymore, but for the majority that I am aware of, it does. Sure, it's up to us dudes to initiate the first contact, to express an interest, and more often then not, to make the first move. But the end result is at the choice of the woman. Not surprisingly though, some women will initiate the first contact. No, I don't mean she'll drop a hankie - that went out with button shoes after women discovered that most men don't understand subtle hints. If a lady sees a guy that appeals to her, she very well could just walk up and start talking to him. Take it for just that - conversation. It doesn't mean she's "loose", promiscuous or that she wants to "match thighs" with a guy, it just means she is interested in the guy. She will also know whether there is a mutual interest in return.

Women have this incredible instinct, I haven't figured out where it comes from, but none the less it's there. They know what a man is up to. Has your own mother ever known what you were up to, or what you were doing, <u>before</u> you did? How she knew when you were coming in late when you were supposed to be home earlier? It isn't a 'mom' thing, this applies to <u>all</u> women. To those men who are, or have been married, how is it that your wife knows when you're coming home with a snoot full of beer? Or if you've been out swinging through the trees and barking at the moon? This instinct, wherever it comes from, can vary from woman to woman. Some have an incredible amount. Almost scary. Maybe all women are psychic, as they sure as hell know when a man is going to get laid. They also know when a man is 'eyeballing' them, or undressing them with their eyes. Whether you believe it or not, a lot of women have this ability to sense what men have been doing, are doing and going to do.

In the never ending quest of romance for both sexes, women need and want men as much as we men want them. You would be surprised at some of the things I've overheard from women talking about men. I've heard them talking in grocery stores, bars, at the post office, at parties, you name it. Maybe that's why they go to the restroom in 'groups', to sort of compare notes. Maybe that's a girl thing, but if some guy said to me, "Let's go to the men's room", I'd tell him that he better go by himself, then spend the rest of time making sure I never turned my backside to him.

None the less, women do talk about men. I've had some pretty strange things said to me by women about their men, and some were downright intimate. Like I was some sort of clearing house for relationship problems or something. There have also been some pretty lame statements made by men about women. Some men have a real weird concept of dealing with women, and some of them would make a rational person raise their eyebrows. As for some things I have been told or overheard from men, it seems there are some fellas out and around that, in my opinion, should not be allowed in public without supervision. Some guys just don't have clue about women, yet they think they are the 'cock of the walk'. If common sense were to be measured in units of gasoline, there wouldn't be enough to power a piss-ants go cart around the inside of a Cheerio. For the most part, these men apparently haven't paid much attention to their surroundings. I've seen plants that had more sense. By the same token, I've known some women that had an IQ of three below a fence post and if a single thought were to enter their mind, it would perish from loneliness.

Most male pursuit of women takes place everywhere, in a nightclub, bar, sports event, social gatherings, etc. I have been to many, by myself or with a lady, but I have always been aware of people and conversations around me. Some of the crap I have heard men say to women have given cause to spilling my beer, if not chuckling silently. The women just either sit there and suck it up, some let him keep ranting, then blow him off like a popcorn fart or shoot him down in flames.

Some men honestly have a low opinion of women and believe that a woman doesn't have the ability or is smart enough to count her boobs and come up with same number twice. My best guess for this attitude is that these guys have low self-esteem and a small penis.

There are things for men to know and understand about women if they ever want romance from them. That's what this book is about. Scratching your gonads, hocking out lugi and farting will not make you a babe magnet. That activity is for hunting and fishing trips, playing football and other guy things.

First, men are basically reactionary thinkers, and women are basically analytical thinkers. I didn't say logical, I said analytical. There is a difference between being logical and analytical, although you'd think that through evolution over the years that the women would figure out how toilet seats operate. Being analytical thinkers compared to logical, here is an example: If a woman wants to buy something, she'll look and compare the item from several different stores. That's analytical. Now if sees an ad from a store that has the same something at $3.00 cheaper, but the store is 50 miles away, she'll go to that store, buy it, and believe she has saved money. But logically she doesn't realize she spent $30.00 in gas money to get there and back. That's the difference. With being analytical in mind, you as a man should be careful as to what you say to a lady in the early stages of a relationship, as she will no doubt try to analyze the meaning of your words or phrases. All women will do this in the beginning, but as she becomes more aware of your expressions, the less she'll be analyzing you.

On the other side, men are not without their weirdness. A good example would be a man will have a 'falling out' with his woman over her cooking, then go out camping with his buddies, eat a half-cooked fish covered with campfire soot, drink coffee made with gritty creek water and call it great. There is nothing known on this planet to alleviate this condition between the male and female brain, so guys and gals, you'll just have to accept it.

The male and female brains, although similar in size, are in fact, very different as I have pointed out. Another oddity thing is the female brain has a large area, about the size of a tennis ball, where emotions are stored. In a woman, this is where a vast amount of emotional information is kept, usually an endless culmination of relationships that are held in suspension for an immeasurable amount of time. The male equivalent of this area of the brain is about the size of a jelly bean, to which contents are made up of recent sports highlights, auto racing, beer commercials and it resets every weekend.

Women, on the other hand, can expound with an in innumerable amount of feelings covering the past 15 years. Men, as a large part, don't express any romantic feelings. Women call this being insensitive. We're not, we do have feelings but sometimes we just don't care to reveal them. Period. Also, we see that there is absolutely no reason whatsoever to retain any and all thoughts of previous romances that are no longer, nor do we wish to be compared to any of those past romances of our lady.

With regard to previous romances, if a woman you've had a relationship with comes back into your life and should she want to 'reconnect', then most men simply purge any and all circumstances of past and everything starts over at square one. Women however, will not dispense with what once was, and will retain everything as it was in the relationship. For some reason, their memory banks do not have a delete function. Only thing you can do is try to get her to clean the skeletons out of the closet.

The male and female brains function differently as well as the thought process that I just mentioned. In the male brain, there is a secretion of fluids that allows him to watch more than 4 football games and 1 or 2 auto races on several TV's all at the same time, and tell you the score of each game, the lead car in a race plus all the beer commercials that were aired.

The female brain however, produces a chemical from time to time that causes them to believe they have an inadequate number of shoes. This difference in brain matter will always be there. The male and female brains will never operate on the same frequency, speed, or on the same principles. I can only guess The Almighty designed that way.

Women, as a general rule, like men to do things for them. Sure, they talk about being independent, able to think for themselves, self-sufficient, etc., but they still enjoy a man to do the niceties. Simple stuff, like opening doors for them, light their cigarettes, offer up their seat if there is none available, pour her drink, etc. Of course, you have the minor percentage that wants to do everything by her self, trash talk men, and scream equality. I'm not talking about equality. This has nothing to do with 'equality'. That equality crap is something that a few women came up with because they put their bra on backwards one day and it fit better. There are simply some things that men can do better and some things that women can do better – accept it.

As part of the male brain, men should learn to deal with their infamous ego. A treacherous creature, that lies within all men and is more often than not, their own downfall – if they do not control it. Egos have their purpose, but it should not be allowed to totally override a man's thoughts or actions. There is a balance there somewhere, and its up to every man to find it. A woman likes a man to be assertive, confident, bold, and at the same time, compassionate and sensitive. They look for strength – not just physical, but emotional strength as well. It's all related to her maternal instinct that motivates her to selecting a mate, to father her offspring. Don't go around like Attila the Hun but don't be some milk-toast panty-waist idiot either. Like I said, there is a balance.

Women also have egos, or to be more specific, vanity. Ever notice they can't stand to see another woman wearing the same outfit as they have on. They have to have shoes that match their purse and a purse that match their eyes. They spend more than the national debt on shoes and cosmetics. They pluck their eyebrows, some have their boobs fluffed up a size or two and some even shave their clam, but they all judge one another by the clothes, size of their boobs, size of their butt, hairdo, and the amount of makeup. Ever wonder why sea going ships are referred to as 'she', 'her', etc.? To coin a phrase by a Navy Admiral, it's because it costs a lot to keep them in paint and powder.

It all comes down to the fact that they want to look 'attractive', and, to feel good about themselves. Not only to the opposite sex, but to other women as well. It's some sort of 'competition' between women. Have you ever noticed that when a woman walks into a room, that the other women will look her up and down as if to 'check her out', then one or the other will make eye contact with the other as if to send the message "Cheap Trash!"

In a sense, us men are the same way, although we don't wear makeup or shave our pubic hair. Those of you who do, I don't want to know about. We all groom ourselves, some shave or grow a beard of sorts, maintain long hair, short hair, or no hair, use deodorant and cologne, etc. We dress to fit the occasion, or we dress to what we want to wear. Men do this to be comfortable, to feel good about our attire, and to make ourselves appealing to women. But unlike women, we do not give a tinker what other men think or care about the way we ourselves look. What we wear is what we want to wear, and if other guys don't like it, well, they can put their opinion where the sun don't shine.

Unlike women, who have their 'assets' somewhat visible in size and shape, a man's self-appointed 'asset-supreme' is hidden from day to day view. The penis. His love muscle, moisture-missile, turtle, one-eyed worm, etc., regardless of what term you use, some men dwell on the size of their weenie. Some men even give names to their prized appendage. Men in the restroom will even take a peak in the next urinal to see how the other fella is fixed for size and compare it to his own, right down to a quarter of an inch. With some guys, it's an obsession. I've heard some women say size doesn't matter, and I've heard some women say size does matter. Somehow, I'd bet money on being given the choice, all women would prefer the large economy size. Ok, so there's a dude who has a sausage that hangs between his knees, and maybe some women oohh and aahh over that, but the fact is, they'd be scared of the damage it could do. The average oyster will only take 6 or 7 inches, and if you try and bury any more then you'll be hitting her uterus and causing her discomfort, even pain.

Now, if your chubby is only 6 inches long but has the diameter of a cucumber, she'll love it. There is an exercise men can do that will somewhat increase the size of their male member, pretty much similar to an exercise a woman can do to tighten up her oyster, but I'm not writing this to give you an exercise program. Anyway fellas, surveys and research by many in the medical field have stated that it only takes 2 inches of penetration to bring a woman to climax. Unlike women who can increase their boob sizes with implants, men can't enlarge the size of their willie with implants. There are a lot of 'additives' on the market that claim to "increase the size of your trophy" but I for one don't believe in that.

If you're a grown adult male, your body has done all the growing it's going to do. Sure you can work out and build up your arms, legs and other muscles, but that's just it – those are muscles. Your tube isn't a muscle, it's an appendage of tissue containing two arteries and the size of which during intimacy, is controlled by blood flow. So save your money guys, and don't believe those advertisements. There are herbs and natural organic substances that will 'enhance' your level of performance, but as for claims of adding 3 or 4 inches, I wouldn't bet the outhouse door on any of them. Best you can do is to keep your arteries clean and maintain healthy blood flow. This is best done by simply watching your diet, get some degree of physical exercise and plenty of rest. Another thing is to watch your intake of alcohol. Doesn't matter whether it's just beer, mixed drinks or wine, too much jungle juice will definitely limit your performance on the playing field.

The bottom line is, unless your love sausage isn't any bigger than a doorstop for a dollhouse, you shouldn't be overly concerned with it.

Chapter Two

Attraction

All through our daily lives, we all see a woman that appeals to us, that we'd like to meet and get to know, and yes, get in bed. Well, the same goes for the women, but we're going to deal with you dudes out there. I myself have seen many a lady that I would really like to get next to. Some I did, some I didn't. Among those that I didn't, was primarily because they were sporting an obvious band of metal on their left hand, and many years ago I learned that a smart monkey doesn't monkey with another monkeys' monkey.

Those of you who consider it a challenge, or do it anyway, I trust your health insurance is paid up. I doubt you would like it if some dude was hitting on your lady. I've even seen men hit on a woman that was with her boyfriend or husband. I realize there are some men who will do it anyway and continue to try and hit on a married woman but again I would like to bring to your attention once again, to the health insurance matter.

For those of you married men who try to woo the single women, what the hell do you think you're doing anyway? I couldn't count the number of wedding bands that I've seen suddenly disappear when a married guy sees attractive women. Don't you think that your little lady can't tell when you've been out swinging through the trees and barking at the moon? Sure she can – bet on it! This goes back to the instinct I mentioned earlier. Here's another thought – in this day and age with all the infections in the world, do you want to take home a 'surprise' to your lady? You could very easily contract something that there is no cure for. How'd you like to wake up one morning and find it laying on the floor?

But if you insist on trying to accumulate stains on your underwear, go ahead, but as the saying goes, "Lonely women make good lovers", and while you're out playing around, there just might be some 'Friendly Henry' warming up your bed. After all, most of what makes a woman cheat is lack of attention from her own man.

Lets say you're single and you see a lady that you would really like to meet, to get to know, someone that you are really attracted to. First thing is, be your self. Women will spot a Flaky Jake, but then again, some like that – something about they "can change him". More about "changing the man" is mentioned in chapter three.

I've even noticed that with some women, you could put them in a room with 99 men, all of whom are attractive, perfect gentlemen, employed, upstanding and morally straight, virtually pillars of mankind, then throw in one unemployed, lazy, sleazy, free-loading flaming asshole, and within 30 minutes, she'll find that flaming asshole and want to home with him. Women like that, I recommend that you run away from, as they have loser written all over them.

So you find a woman that is appealing to you. Maybe you have your own line that you've perfected, and maybe it's worked, but not all women respond to "lines". This goes back to being your self. Be honest. Don't come up with some corny phrase or make some silly-ass statement that your buddy told you about. Listening to your buddy's tales of love is sure-fire failure, and probably means your buddy does nothing more than take a lot of soapy showers. I have learned that when guys continuously expound with all of their female exploits, it's all bullshit and the closest they ever get to any pussy is petting a cat. So just be your own self. When the moment comes that you want to ask her out for a date, don't mumble, speak out. If you have a fear of being rejected, you got to realize that in this day and age there is a need for caution. You can see that by watching the news or reading the newspaper, so if she says 'no' initially, let her get to know you first. After all, it could very well mean that she hasn't had enough time to consider things. By your asking, she may feel pressured into giving you an answer, and she would rather take time to get to know you and for her to examine what her own thoughts are. You will be able to tell by her actions towards you to know if it's time to ask her again. However, should she say something other than yes, she means no. "Maybe sometime" means no, "I'll call you sometime" means no, "I've been really busy lately" means no, "You're really nice, but......" means no, "I'm sort of seeing somebody right now" means no, so on, and so on, and so on. Anything other than yes means no. If she pulls the old "just friends" routine on you, this translation most likely means "I like you, I like the attention, but I have no further interest in you, about you, or for you". This is usually to keep you on the back burner but is still on the lookout for Mr. wonderful to come along. It's up to you if you want to keep spinning your wheels, or to fold your tent and get in the wind.

Back to the first encounter, eye contact and a smile is sufficient. If she responds in the same manner, then there's the start. If she doesn't, don't even think of taking it any further. If you do, all you're doing is putting her on the spot, which will usually result in you going down in flames, and you are also making an ass out of yourself. If you push it anyway, you were already a supreme asshole to start with.

So let's say she responds in a positive manner. The initial intro of dialogue is up to you. Again, be honest. Let her know that you are interested . But in no way should you try to impress her with your worldly achievements, either real or not. Keep it simple. Let her develop a 'comfort level' with you as to how much she wants to know or talk about. Let her lead the conversation. If she doesn't, well homie, she probably isn't that interested, and your best bet at this point in time <u>would</u> be to 'fold your tent and get in the wind'.

Should she have an interest, and you walk away, she just might wonder. Why did he give up? Why did he just walk away? Remember now, this was a girl that responded positive initially to your glance. Women like a certain mystique in a guy. This puts the ball in her court, so to speak. If she wants to, and <u>only</u> if she wants to, she will seek you out for further conversation.

Let's say you and the lady are engaged in conversation. You need to pay attention here, as what she may say in the first minutes of conversation will tell you what kind of woman she is. If within the first sweep of the second hand, she asks you what kind of work you do, that should run the first flag up the pole. Not that you shouldn't tell her, mind you, and she may honestly want to know what you do for a living. However, if that question comes out within the first 30 seconds or so of conversation, and is immediately followed by "What kind of vehicle do you drive", then followed by "Where do you live", then beware - she is most likely nothing but a gold digger. By answering those three questions, you have given her a good idea of how much money you have. Run do not walk, away from her.

Sure, eventually a woman will want to know what you drive, and where you live, but as I said, if those 3 questions come out within the first 1 to 5 minutes, she's more than likely looking for a sugar daddy on a gravy train. Go after her if you want, but keep in mind that when your well runs dry, she'll dump you like a dirty shirt and go find someone else.

Back to the initial conversation. The above hasn't happened, and everything is golden so far. Do not monopolize the conversation. Let her speak, and while she's talking, watch her body language. Ok, so you don't speak femineez - neither did I for a long time. It's easy. I'm only going to touch the surface on this subject, and point out the very obvious basics. These are some very basic things you should look for when talking to her and while she is talking to you.

1. Eye contact. Is she looking at you, or is her head swiveling scanning like a radar grid around the room for someone else to blow her skirt up? If she is looking at you, fine. If not, best to disengage, you're wasting your time and effort.

2. If, after a while and a given amount of conversation, she starts looking away from you or facing away from you, she has changed her mind

(they do that a lot) and wants you to 'fold your tent and get in the wind. Maybe something about you that she decided she doesn't like, or she spotted another blip on her radar.

3.   If she is facing you, but with both her arms crossed in front of her, indicates a defensive posture. That's a barrier indication. Not a challenge, a barrier. If she is sitting with both arms crossed but at a 90 degree angle from you, indicates somewhat of a defensive attitude, but it is a small barrier. Another defensive indicator is if she faces you and crosses her legs, although not as strongly as arms crossed. If she does both, get the hell away from her before she kicks you in the goal post.

4.   Now here's a positive sign. If she is looking at you, smiling, and playing with her hair, she is very much interested in you. If you observe this, maintain yourself and do not start snorting or peeing on the furniture. She has in interest in you so just stay your course. Don't start thinking "you've got her", because she can change to item three above in a New York minute. Let her create the next level.

5.   She's standing in front of you with her hands on her hips, head slightly cocked to one side or back. This is the 'challenge posture' or as if to say "now what are your going to do", or if she feels she has you over a barrel. She is putting you on defense. You're on your own with how you deal with it, since you obviously did or said something of a faux pas to make her react that way.

Those are the most basic of signs, don't try to read anything into anything else a woman may or may not do if you are not a graduate of female body language. Do not try to second-guess her.

I'm sure you've heard things about what a woman looks for in a guy, stuff like being a gentleman, sense of humor, kind, honest, and (here's the kicker) "looks aren't important". Fellas, it would be easier to move Moses off the mountain before I will <u>ever</u> believe that! Face it, if a guy isn't at <u>least</u> half way attractive, a woman isn't going to talk to him long enough to find out what kind of personality he has, let alone if he is kind, gentle, and has a sense of humor! Sorry ladies, you've been exposed, so you might as well admit it that looks <u>do</u> in fact play a major part.

Chapter Three

The Relationship

Now we go to the part about you and your lady are "seeing each other", living together, engaged, he'n & she'n, or whatever. Usually at this point, is where the woman will try to "change" the man, for whatever reason. Some women will deny this, but they <u>all</u> do it – to some degree or another, whether conscious or subconscious doesn't matter, but they all do it. How much effort they put into it will depend on much they feel the need to 'be in control' of the relationship. I haven't figured out why they go through this phase, but they do.

When this occurs, one of four things results from her efforts: One, she succeeds in changing the guy to be what she perceives as <u>the</u> perfect man, then steps back and wonders what happened to the man she fell in love with. Two, she tries, does not succeed in changing him, accepts it, and life goes on. Three, she tries, does not succeed, then chucks the relationship to go find some milk-toast jerk she <u>can</u> control. Which, by the way, is the reason I'm not married any more.

And finally, four; she tries, does not succeed, then makes the guys life so miserable that he leaves her, thus earning him the title of *"The Asshole"*.

Once this change phase has passed, and life as you know it continues, then you need to realize some additional factors about your sweetie. The "points system" she uses.

All women have their own points system that they use with their fella. Based on math, some are simple, some are lengthy, and some are harder to figure out than Japanese arithmetic. None the less, they are there and it is up to you as a man to know and abide by her system. Doesn't mean you understand it, it just means you are aware of it. Any attempt to modify or any deviation from her system, could result in burnt meals, no sex, and generally be hazardous to your overall wellbeing.

This merit/demerit system will vary from woman to woman, and the pluses and minus depend on her own creativity. In the world of romance, one single rule applies: Make the woman happy. Do something she likes and you get points. Do something she doesn't like and points are subtracted. You don't however, get any points for doing something she expects. Again, the system varies from one woman to the next, but I have written here a few examples of the most notable that I've observed. Numeric value is not a standard mind you, but the idea is to give you some sort of indication of how it works.

Simple examples

You make the bed.. +1
you make the bed, but forget to fluff the pillows .... -1
you throw the bedspread over rumpled sheets .... -2
You leave the toilet seat up .... -5
You replace the roll of toilet paper when its out 0
You go out & buy her extra-light panty liners with wings +5

in the snow .... +8
and return with beer .... -5
and no liners.. -25

You check out a suspicious noise at night..........................0
you check out a suspicious noise at night and it is nothing .0
you check out a suspicious noise at night and it is
something... +5
you pummel it with a bat .... +10
it's her cat.. -40

You go out to a party and stay at her side the entire night ...0
You stay with her for awhile, then leave to chat with a college
friend .... -2
named Crystal .... -20
Crystal is a dancer.. -30
with breast implants .... -50

You remember her birthday 0
with a card...0
with flowers... +2
with a card, flowers and take her out to dinner............... +10
it's not a sports bar .... +5
it is a sports bar .... -2
it's all-you-can-eat night .... -5

You go out with friends for a boys night out 0
they're all married... +1
they're all single.. -10

You take her to a movie .... +2
it's a movie she likes.. +4
it's a movie you don't like .... +6

it's a movie you like .... -2
you lied and said it was a foreign film about orphans ...... -15

You develop a pot belly .... -15
you exercise to get rid of it 10
you resort to loose jeans and baggy pants to hide it .... -30
you tell her "So what, you have one too .... -100

You hesitate in responding when she asks if a dress makes her look fat .... -10
you reply "Where .... -30
you reply "No, I think it's your ass .... -200
any other response .... -5

You display an attentive expression when she talks to you .0
you listen to her for over 30 minutes .... +5
you relate to her conversation with a similar situation of your own .... +50
your mind wanders and then she says "Well, what do you think?" .... -100
you change the subject or fall asleep .... -200

You talk to her when she's having her period .... -200
you don't talk to her… .... -200
you spend time with her .... -200
you don't spend time with her .... -200
any other activity or dialogue .... -200

These are but a few examples that a woman uses with her points system. Learn from it, and live by it, because as I have mentioned before, your sanity may depend on it.

Right now, you're probably thinking that it's a one-way street for men, and that the women are free from understanding and learning that men also, have requirements that should be recognized. Men are simple creatures, and have simple needs. There are three things every man should have: A good woman, a good dog and ready cash. We don't have complex lives like women, and most of our activity involves simple things. So, advising your woman about the male requirements, it will ensure her that her needs, wants and desires will be complied with if she is willing to accept certain things with you as a man.

For starters, all men need to advise their women of some things, such as men do not think of shopping as a sport. Never have, and never will. As a general rule, if a man wants to buy something, he already knows what he wants, goes to the store, buys it, and departs. Hanging around in the sporting goods department does not qualify as the term 'shopping'.

Remind her that men only see in the seven colors of the light spectrum. For example, peach is a fruit, not a color. Pumpkin is a vegetable, not a color. Tan is what you get by being out in the sun. Furthermore, you should tell your lady that we men have no idea what fuchsia is.

One thing that all men should reiterate to their lady is, don't ask a question that is misleading or that can be interpreted in more that one way. That's entrapment. Most of all, a woman should not ask: "Do you think I'm fat?" If she has to ask, she probably is.

Another thing your women should realize is that if they want something, ask! Little hints do not work. Big hints do not work. Most men wouldn't recognize a hint to begin with if they stepped in it, so get her to just <u>say</u> what's on her mind.

The silent treatment women emulate from time to time is a waste of good oxygen. If a man asks a woman what's wrong, she'll say "nothing". Duh. Ok, we're all dumb males but not that dumb. You'll know something is bugging her, but if she isn't not going to tell you, then you can't fix it.

Last, men need to tell your women that she should understand that anything said by a man 6 months ago is inadmissible in an argument. (they try this a lot) But women need to realize that all comments become null and void after 7 days. Speaking of arguments, men should be advised that there are two theories to arguing with a woman and neither works. Therefore fellas, never pass up a good chance to just shut up. Remember, good judgment comes from experience, and a lot that comes from bad judgement.

Chapter Four

What You Can Do To Please Her

This chapter is pretty simple. Earlier, I mentioned that women like to see the compassionate and sensitive side to a guy's makeup as well as the other things that attract them to us males. This doesn't mean you have to chuck your macho masculinity fellas, it just means that if you want to earn her admiration, you need to stop spitting, pawing at the ground and scratching your nuts once in a while. The occasional realignment of expression is painless, will not ruin your image at the sports bar and the results can be immeasurable. It doesn't take a whole lot of effort on your part, and by doing such, your relationship will flourish.

I have listed here some things a man could do to win the admiration of his lady. How often you choose to perform these expressions is up to you, and the more often the better. Don't think you can make it an annual event only and expect and lasting results from her, it doesn't work that way. Learn to develop a sensitive nature <u>along</u> with your masculinity, show her that she is important. By this, I don't mean it's ok just say "You're the apple of my eye honey", then scratch your balls and reach for the TV remote. That's the way-wrong approach nimrod, and if you think it's enough, that it's all she needs, well then, don't be surprised of her attitude towards you. For example, if you were to say "Honey, lets switch positions tonight," she's liable to say "Ok, you do the dishes and take care of the laundry and I'll sit on the couch and fart." With that, she's telling you to 'spank your own monkey'. If you want your woman to please you, then dude, you've got to please her. The door swings both ways.

For the most part, women are sensitive to "little things" from a man. For example, putting little notes in her purse. You can simply write I Love You, or, you can write an intimate suggestive remark. Be creative. You can leave these notes anywhere - in her car, on her pillow, in her purse, in the dresser drawer where she keeps her bras and panties, or just about anywhere. If she's out shopping or at work, put a single rose on her pillow before she comes home. If you have some extra coupons in the bank account, then rent the side of billboard that she passes every day. I knew a guy who did this and it was just an expression of a romantic moment between the two of them. Another thing (that's not so expensive), record your voice on a cassette or CD and refer to intimacy between the both of you, and be specific. Then stop by her place of work and tell her to listen to it when she leaves work. Depending on the intimacy content of the recording you made for her, by the time she gets home she just might very well be sticking to the upholstery and drooling all over herself. Use your imagination.

Here is the list of some of the things men can do, not in any specified order or importance, to please his lady, to win her heart and admiration.

> Be kind to her.
> Be considerate of her.
> Be understanding of her.
> Listen to her – what she has to say is important to her.
> Walk beside her – not in front of her, nor behind her.

Treat her as your equal.
Give her attention.
Compliment her.
Show her you care.
Let her know she is important.
Make her feel 'special'.
Open doors for her.
Respect her feelings.
Respect her thoughts.
Respect her wishes.
Accept her opinion.
Talk to her, with her.
Ask for her thoughts.
Offer To help her with chores.
Rub her feet, her neck & shoulders.
Hold her hand.
Remember certain dates.
Give or send her small presents, notes or flowers.

Some women may think that this chapter isn't long enough, well girls, depends on just how self centered you are. It's a 2 way street ladies, and you would do well to remember that. Anyway, these expressions of a mans' sensitivity isn't limited to just what is listed here, so if you guys can think of more, then by all means, use them.

Above all, what you should <u>not</u> do, is ogle other women while you're with her. <u>She</u> should be the center of your attention. You can drool, scratch and sniff all you want when you're with your buddies, and it doesn't matter if you should finding your self getting an appetite - just make sure you do your eating at home.

Chapter Five

What She Can Do To Please You

Show up naked and bring beer.

Chapter Six

Sex and Making Love

How many of you homies went straight to this chapter first? Quite a few I'll bet, now go back to the beginning and read what I wrote in the first few chapters so you will better understand what I wrote in this chapter.

This department is where most men do not have any idea whatsoever, other than satisfying their own physical needs. Most men believe they are adequate lovers in pleasuring their woman. They're wrong. A lot of women have let it be known that this department is where their sweetie is lacking, or doesn't satisfy them. I would be willing to bet that a very small percentage of men really know how to please a woman sexually. Sorry guys, but there is more to making love than copulation.

Atypical scenario: The average man, in the desire for sex, starts with a little cuddling, a kiss or two here and there, then by longer and deeper kissing, followed with the grabbing and rubbing of the boobs, maybe a little nibbling of the nipples while the finger or fingers fondles and probes her clam. This scenario on the average lasts for about 3 to 4 minutes, plus or minus a minute. Next, Mr. U-Boat Commander submerges his submarine, conducts several dives, and within two minutes, he shoots his torpedoes then pops back up to the surface. Then, with a peck of a kiss, he jumps up, beats his chest, throws grass & leaves in the air, and he's off to the refrigerator, or he simply rolls over and goes to sleep. Either case, he is leaving his woman lying there wondering what the hell just happened. Now unlike the rodeo, 8 seconds is <u>not</u> a good ride! If making love is viewed as 3 or 4 minutes of groping and heavy breathing, then you're obviously not the brightest light in the harbor.

Men should realize that women need, require and want foreplay. It's kind of like taking a cruise ship – getting there is half the fun. Another thing, women complain about is very rarely will a man utter a word or any other intelligible sound during sex. C'mon guys, you're both laying there, completely naked, everything is out in the open, and you're silent. I realize that the Almighty gave a man two heads but with only enough blood to run one at a time, however I know for a fact that the vocal cords still function. <u>Talk</u> to her! That's right, communicate! Let her know how you feel, what you think, how she makes you excited, so on and so on and so on. Tell her that you want to know what <u>she</u> wants, what gives <u>her</u> pleasure, what <u>she</u> likes, and so forth. This isn't a sign of you being inept or not knowing what you're doing, it's being responsive to her.

Once again, each and every woman is different. They don't come with a standard blueprint, or a generic nomenclature that everything operates the same on all models. All women have different likes and dislikes when it comes to making love. Because they don't want to crush the male ego, women are reluctant to speak out about their wants, likes and so forth – simply because they don't want to hurt the guys' feelings. So if you guys can just disconnect your ego, open up and communicate to her. That alone will ease any feelings of her being apprehensive in telling you anything. You first need to establish a certain 'comfort' level for her. Once you've done this, you'll be surprised of the amore that she displays. Remember - <u>talk</u> to her, let her become 'comfortable', and give her all the foreplay she wants!

Having sex shouldn't be limited to the bedroom. Nor should it be 'scheduled'. Making love in places or spots other than the bed can be very arousing. Even the bathtub, or the kitchen table. If you want to get more adventurous, then there's always semi-public sex. In the park, in a car, on a picnic or in the backyard. Just make sure that there isn't any "Do-Right Boys" (police) near by, because if they see you, they won't know if you're assaulting her or just being "friendly".

Anyway, sex doesn't have to be confined to one room, one area, or any timetable. Furthermore, it shouldn't be a constant set pattern. By this I mean, don't always follow the same routine. Do something different each time. This alone will create a level of excitement in her, as to 'what is he going to do next'. Making love doesn't always have to be serious neither. You can make it funny, tasty, adventurous and depending on the two of you, you can use various array of items. For example, lace her entire body with the petals of a rose, or a feather plume. But don't use the whole bird, that's getting kinky - unless you both are into the kinky stuff. You can paint her in chocolate syrup or whipped cream, then lick it all off. Buy her some of those edible panties; they come in various flavors such as cherry, grape, orange and so on, but I don't think they make them with beer flavoring. Use your imagination, it'll give you both a memorable time.

In the process of foreplay, a fella may find that he derives as much pleasure from it as much as she does. The more foreplay a guy does and the more time he takes to arouse her, then the better the sex for both, not to mention that it will get you both hotter than the surface of the sun. When the time is right, go ahead and slip it in, but ever so slowly. Not all the way, just a little bit, then slowly pull it out and rub it against her clitoris. Do this a few times until she can't stand it anymore. You probably can't either. Now you're off to euphoria, and feel free to make all the unintelligible sounds you want, the more, the better she'll enjoy you and knows you are enjoying her. Who knows, she just may chime in and vocalize along with you, but I wouldn't focus on harmonizing. A mans' duration of performance during intercourse will depend on his stamina, health and ability, so you guys would do well to take care of yourself.

Regarding oral sex, this depends entirely on the both of you and her and personal attitude. Women have different feelings about 'going down on a man'. Some like it, some don't. If she doesn't, then don't push it. Most likely, if she doesn't like bobbing your apple, there isn't a whole lot you can do to change her mind. Sure, she may do it just to make you happy but she herself won't like it one bit. It's up to you if you want to create this situation, but I personally wouldn't recommend it. Some women don't want to polish your knob but they will enjoy you grazing between her thighs. It's up to the both of you to define the playground. Whatever it may or may not be, do not push her to something she is not comfortable with.

Lets say she wants to take your penis in her mouth, this is a great turn on for some women. Whether you choose to shoot in her mouth, or just let her 'fluff you up' for intercourse, is up to the two of you. She may even want you to 'pull out' during intercourse, so she can take your tube in her mouth. Some women like the taste of their own juices.

Sometimes, when actual intercourse is not preferred, such as her period, then masturbation for both of you can be performed. Some women enjoy watching a man masturbate, and will eagerly show them how they themselves do it. Some women will want to 'take the matter in hand' and do it for you. Or, she may want you to put your sausage between her boobs, and stroke along until you shoot. This is better known as 'giving her a pearl necklace'. So if you are, or she is pulling your pork, go ahead and squirt on her. Some women like to feel a man's semen on them, especially on their boobs or their face. Besides, it is one of the best things that a woman can do for her complexion is to have a man's semen on her face, after all, it's 100% protein. Same with the juice from a woman. If you don't believe it, check with a dermatologist. If they don't agree, then my guess is they're opinionated and don't like oral sex themselves.

Whatever form of making love you choose, after you've squirted the baby batter, don't just get off & up. Leave your sausage in her wrapper. A lot of women find it incredibly romantic if you stay inside her. Talk to her. Using a good bedside manner, you should use "pillow talk", whisper sweet nothings and so forth. But what ever you refer to, do not bring up the evening news, football standings, auto racing or the like. How would you feel if she started talking about the sale down at the shopping mall? Just keep it to "pillow talk". Give her soft and light kisses to her ears, lips, eyebrows, neck, forehead, nose, talk some more, then more kisses. Again, you guys just might realize you enjoy it as much as she does. In fact, do it long enough, and you might just find that there's a replay coming up. Remember - resort to "pillow talk" with her. In any case, <u>do</u> <u>not</u> ask the nimrod question of "Was it good for you too?" If you've followed the guidelines I've written, you won't have to - you'll know by her display of affection toward you afterwards. For one thing, if nothing else, you'll know by the shit-eating grin on her face!

Chapter Seven

Her Erogenous Zones

There are more erogenous zones on a woman's body than most of them probably realize they have. These zones, or areas, are specific parts on a woman that stimulate her arousal for sex. Some women have more, but I have listed those that are specifically known and identified areas. When a man takes the time to 'light these up', you will introduce her a level of arousal she didn't know was attainable. I'll go into these erogenous zones in a minute. This effort of 'turning her wick up', or call it lift off, if the man does so, may occupy about 30 minutes to an hour. This doesn't mean you have a minimum and a maximum time zone, it depends on the guy, the girl and the situation.

Some women may have 'mental blocks' so to speak about some of them, but none the less, they will stimulate her to some degree or another. By mental blocks, I refer to certain areas that they may consider 'yuk', or unorthodox, or taught at an early age as a no-no. If should you encounter this, again resort to talking. You need to reassure her that it is nothing Ju-Ju about them and that she should try to 'let go' and enjoy the stimulation. If she doesn't, don't push it. You want her comfort level established, not walled up.

These are some of the areas that will arouse her. Remember, all women respond differently to various parts of their body and there is no 'roadmap' that applies to all, and if the communication link is established, she'll tell you what she likes. Anyway, here are the most common ones.

Most obvious, her boobs. A common myth about a woman's boobs is their size, in that big boobs are less sensitive than smaller boobs. Size has nothing to do with their sensitivity. However, time of the month does.

Don't squeeze them hard, you're not kneading dough. Most women enjoy a mans' hands on their boobs, so squeeze them gently, firmly but not roughly. Caress them. I once knew a lady who told me her boobs were so sensitive, she could have an orgasm simply by a man touching and caressing them.

Her nipples. Some women like to have you rub them gently between your thumb and forefinger. If you do, make sure your digits are wet. Simply lick them before you touch her nipples. Lace you tongue around her nipples with your tongue, in a circle, then breathe lightly on them. Use your lips on them, but not your teeth. Breathing on them will make them 'peak' and a when her nipples are 'peaked', they are at their maximum sensitivity.

Another area is her forehead. Just kiss it gently and tenderly. If you rub it, do it gently, it's not a football. Her temples can also be a pleasure zone.

Lace your fingertips gently on the inside of her elbows and upper arms, this will give her a tickling and, a tingling sensation. Kiss her there as well.

A relatively unknown area is her armpits. Yea, her armpits. Unless she just finished a workout, there's nothing gross about it. Kiss around them, lightly rub them.

Her eyebrows and eyelids are another area, kiss her there.

Her ears, neck and shoulders. Touch, kiss, caress and breathe lightly.

The nape, or back of her neck; again kiss, lick and breathe on it.

Run your tongue down her spine, to the small of her back. There are tiny hairs there that are like sensual antennas. Lick, and again breathe lightly.

Caress her buns using the very tips of your fingers.

The backs of her thighs. Again, use your fingertips gently and lightly. Use your tongue as well and breathe softly.

The backs of her knees as well. Lick her legs all the way to her ankles. Rub her feet. The insides of her thighs near her clam is another very nice place for your tongue to visit. It will create a lot of hip movement from her in anticipation.

Her tummy, just above her clam is another sensual spot. Run your fingertips very lightly there, and kiss, lick and breathe lightly.

You should linger for a while at all these areas, and then return from time to time.

Her oyster.

Gently but firmly rub the full length of it at first. To stimulate her clitoris, rub it in a circular motion (this is how most women masturbate). Your finger or thumb should be wet or well lubricated, and don't rub hard, it's not a lottery scratch ticket. Let her be your guide as to how much and how fast to rub. If you're into going down on a woman as most men are, use your tongue in a circular motion first, then side to side. Don't cover her clitoris with your lips, this smothers the sensation. Use only your tongue, slightly pointed, lightly flicking from side to side. While you're grazing on the lower pasture, she may want you to insert a finger or fingers in her oyster. Go ahead, but best make sure your hands and nails are clean. You could cause an infection in her.

One side of her clitoris is more sensitive than the other, so just flick your tongue side to side. If you become tired, you can hold you tongue steady and just move your head side to side. The longer you do this, it eventually will bring her to orgasm and you'll end up looking like a glazed donut. When she achieves an orgasm, it doesn't mean she done. Women can have more than one orgasm and in some cases can have multiple orgasms, one right after another. Women also have different levels or intensities of orgasms from stimulation, but all women get the most intense pleasure from copulation. Sure, they enjoy having orgasms from stimulation and orgasms from oral sex, but most all women will tell you that <u>nothing</u> beats the pleasurable feeling more than the penetration of a mans' penis.

Her 'G' spot. To stimulate her 'G-spot', keep the palm of your hand up, insert your finger in her with knuckle side down. It's located about 2 inches in, and on the upper side.

It's a rather rough area, almost like a callous, if you have trouble finding it, let her guide you along. Once you've located it, gently assert rubbing pressure against it. Some women have said they've had the most intense orgasm from this stimulation, and some women say they don't. It may not be easy to find, and she herself may not know where it is, so no need to make a career of locating it.

Each woman is different and will respond differently to these areas. Some women will have a higher sensitivity in one area than another woman. She will tell you. Here we go back to communication. Use it!

These zones, should be used not only during foreplay, but in the afterglow of intercourse as well. If you guys can 'program yourselves' to these principles, your sessions of passion could possibly consume from 1 to 3 hours, depending on you, your efforts, and your lady. Whatever the time frame, remember fellas, a woman does not have an auto ignition switch. They require time to get the motor running and the fire burning. They also would like very much to have a slow and gentle cool down, or re-entry. Do this with your lady and you will enjoy her more and she will enjoy you more, and you can take that to the bank.

Now this doesn't mean that every time you have sex that you'll have to adhere to lengthy foreplay. Women get horny just as men do - only they suppress their horns better than men do. There will be times that your lady gets a rumbling in her loins and will want to climb in the sheets and play the bedspring symphony with you and with very little arousing needed from you. She'll let you know when she's ready to just 'get it on'.

If you've been together as a couple for a while, here's another something that you should know and put in your 'Gee-Whiz' file. I've been told about this 'hidden desire' from many women. There is a goddess in every woman that has this secret abandoned lust of suddenly being ravished by their man. Without instigating anything, without foreplay or anything else, they secretly want their man to instantly just strip her clothes off and 'take her'. To be so overwhelmed with desire for her, right there, right then and right now!

Mind you, if you care to try this barbarian approach and your lady appears anything other than submissive, then don't push it. However, if she appears submissive, then proceed. You should know your lady and what she is responsive to before resorting to the Neanderthal assault.

This is probably better known as 'the quickie', or 'nooner'. But do be ever so mindful of your locale fellas, you don't want to be kicked out of the grocery store.

Again, this display of passion only pertains to couples that have been together for a while or are married. Now if you're not endowed with common sense 101, or unless you have some sort of death wish, I do not recommend you trying this on the first date! Not only would you most likely get both eyeballs slapped over into the same socket, but you just might end up wearing stripes.

Chapter Eight

Fathering A Baby

So you want to have a baby. Well, if you and your lady have decided to have a baby, then I hope it was a well thought out choice and that your relationship is stable, you've both made the commitment of bringing a child into the world, and that you are both financially able. Bringing a child into the world is something that should not be taken lightly, for it is the ultimate challenge of responsibilities. Once the baby is born, your daily and weekly activities will change about 80%. Remember those spur of the moment larks that you and your lady just up and took off to? Gone. Those parties you would have or attend? Limited. Going out to the nightclubs and dancing? Limited. Hanging out with your buddies at the sports bar? Limited. Buying a super entertainment center and other 'toys'? Gone. This is where you had better be financially able because starting with the first year you can count on spending a significant amount of money. It's probably even more expensive nowadays than I encountered. Even with insurance, there's baby furniture, clothes, diapers, baby food, toys, diapers, day care, baby food, medical, diapers, clothes, more toys, diapers, so on, and so on. I remember one young man who told me that he and his girl were getting married and wanted to have a baby. I mentioned the above about money and his reply was that "it couldn't possibly cost that much". He thought all he had to spend was around 2 or 3 hundred dollars. I told him you'll spend <u>more</u> than that on food alone. He couldn't understand how, as he only figured on feeding the baby macaroni & cheese. (there's a kid that would grow up hating the stuff) He also mentioned that he was living with his parents, going to school full time and only worked part time at a grocery store. More than obvious, it became apparent to me that this fella was heading for a sharp learning curve and like the refrigerator, the light only comes on when the door is open. I could only hope that some where along his path, he experiences a wake-up call because Mother Nature is a hard teacher - she gives the test first, then the lessons come later.

Now when the time comes that you both want her to become pregnant, here's some things that you both should be aware of. A woman's ovaries will produce the egg every month, which then travels down to the uterus. Here it stays for a given amount of time, waiting to be fertilized. If it is not, then it passes with her period. She could possibly produce two eggs, thus resulting in twins if fertilized. This egg, or eggs, has no specific sex. It's neither male nor female. The sex of the baby to be will be established from the man's sperm.

The male semen contains both male and female sperm cells that literally swim their way to the uterus. Usually, the female sperm will out-swim the male sperm, as if the uterus was some sort of shopping mall. The male sperm will swim but at a slower pace. With this in mind, and if you both have established a choice of either boy or girl, the man can some what arrange the baby's gender by the depth of penetration at the time of his ejaculation.

If you want a baby girl, then bury it deep when you ejaculate. For a boy, use absolute minimum penetration. A man's sperm will stay alive for a given amount of time, and if there is no egg present, they just may 'hang around' waiting. If you have intercourse one day and the next day an egg appears in her uterus, bingo! Another thing to remember guys, is that while this time the egg is in her uterus, it's known as ovulation, which is when the egg is ready to be fertilized. During this period, the woman's body secrets something that doesn't slow down the female sperm cells, but it increases the speed of the male sperm cells, and instead of just swimming like a fishing trawler, they swim like an 'top fuel drag boat'. This, in conjunction with minimum depth of penetration, will almost guarantee a baby boy. If you want a girl, then dive your submarine to the maximum depth when you squirt. Her G.Y.N. should be able to help determine her ovulation period.

Once it confirmed your lady is pregnant, consider and realize it, as her attitude could possibly change somewhat, and she could possibly develop some cravings for weird things to eat. Some do, some don't. You should remember that she has a new life growing inside her. The things you can and should do is to be attentive and caring. You are the one who created the life that's growing inside her, so you damn well better care about her and that new life! She may or may not be as attentive towards you, but she will want you to express attentiveness towards her. This is only her being maternal. Accept it. Do not do anything to give her a reason to be upset or become mad. Do not go out with the guys and leave her alone at home. Do not expect her to respond to your intimacies, she may or may not. If you or both of you smoke – quit! She should limit her intake of alcohol as well. A couple of beers from time to time is healthy, but not every day. Make sure she eats right. Simply put, no junk food. Her doctor should recommend vitamins she should take. Stay away from pain relievers, prescription drugs and she should not put anything in her body that could affect the baby. Whatever she eats and drinks or otherwise consumes, the baby does also.

Another thing to realize, is that while the baby is growing inside her, that baby is very aware of sound. Voices, music and other noise. Doesn't mean you have to listen to elevator music, but I wouldn't recommend any sound effects from any war movies either. Your voice, and <u>how</u> you talk to your lady will be heard by the baby as well. Remember that! When the time comes for her to deliver the baby, you should be with her. I don't mean in spirit, I mean <u>be</u> there, in the delivery room. Hold her hand, talk to her, after all, you had a hand it this creation. Well, not exactly a "hand", but you know what I mean. Here's another thing that was told to me by a woman doctor, is that the first parent to hold and talk to the baby immediately after childbirth, generally is the person that the baby will have a certain closeness to, for life. Usually it's the baby's mother, but sometimes the baby's father. Regardless, the baby will always have a *special* bond with the mother. I like to think that The Almighty designed it that way.

After the baby is born and home from the hospital, I recommend that you put the baby's crib in your bedroom instead of a room set up for them, for at least the first year. This way, you both will be able to respond more quickly to the baby's needs, whether it's for a feeding or a changing. Also, this will allow the baby to "hear" you both breathing. I'm not sure, but it's been believed that a newborn can actually hear and listen to the parents breathing. This being the case, then the less likely of S.I.D.S. happening. S.D.I.S is defined as Sudden Infant Death Syndrome, where the baby simply stops breathing. So by being able to 'hear' the parents breath, prevents that from happening. Maybe it's true, I don't know, but why chance it – put the baby in your bedroom. Another good reason is so that you don't have to stumble your way through the house in the dark. It is my firm belief that the reason we have toes on our feet is to locate furniture in the dark.

The health and well being of your baby after he or she is born, can and will be the result of you and your lady towards each other, what she eats and drinks and the love you express to each other during her pregnancy.

Once your child is brought into this world, remember this – <u>any</u> man can father a child, but it takes a <u>special</u> kind of man to be a "Dad".

Chapter Nine

Other Things

There are other things that men should know and be aware of about women. Again, there is no manual or blueprint specifications that a man must adhere to, but this is about simple things that would be to a guy's benefit – and happiness. How you apply or accept this, is up to you.

Never, should you vent any anger – of any sort – on a woman! If she does something that displeases you, tell her, but never vent your anger, either physical or verbal. Doing so, places you as the lowest form of life on earth. Besides, I've seen some women that could literally kick the shit out of a man! If you feel you have some macho tough-guy thing to prove, go pick a fight with a thunderstorm or run full speed into a cactus.
(this same ruling applies to children as well, if you haven't figured that out yet)

Do not intentionally embarrass her, or 'put her down', especially in front of other people. Nor should you bring up personal matters about her in front of others. For if you do, it will only give everyone else an impression of you as being a small man – in more ways than one.

If you have a matter of difference, or problem between the both of you, then take her aside, in private, discuss and resolve the issue - before you go out around other people.

Arguments are a fact of life. You and your sweetie are going to have them. Show me a couple that doesn't argue, and I'll show you a couple that doesn't care much about each other. The level of the argument, or intensity, is where you need to <u>maintain</u> your self. This means <u>watch</u> the tone of your voice and the words that you say, because once they're spoken, there's no backspace key. There should never be any physical contact either, or launching of objects aimed at her. Or aimed at anything else, for that matter. The same goes for her as well. Another thing that my dad has told me, and it simply states that if you and you lady are having a high pressure discussion of any magnitude, resolve it. But under no circumstances, you should <u>never go to bed with an argument</u>!! Resolve it. Nobody needs to 'win'. Here's something to keep in mind – there are but three sides to any argument, yours, hers, and the truth.

Doesn't matter who or what is to blame, disagreements happen, whether from opinions, misunderstanding or whatever, what I'm saying is it would be wise for you to diffuse the situation, the best and easiest way possible. Women are emotional creatures, and it is not wise to fuel their wrath. Remember what happened to that one fella? For those who don't remember the newsworthy event in the 1990's, this dude brought untold woe unto himself when his wife - in anger - "shortened his stroke", so to speak. But, with a little luck, a good surgeon & super glue, he got it re-attached.
(I'm kiddin' about the super glue, but you knew that - I hope)
Women can, and will, expound with greater emotional fury than the force of a thunderstorm. Which, I might add, is why hurricanes used to be named after women. Somewhere, the

equality bit snuck into the scene and now hurricanes are named after men as well. Seems odd to me, after all, they don't call them "Himmacanes". So much for the weather report, back to women.

Do not try to control her. She is a person, an individual. You don't want her trying to control you, then don't try to control her. Don't try to tell her what, when, where, how, or with who, she can do things. If you're one of these guys that feels he must, then you're an insecure idiot and you probably have a small penis.

If your lady is not employed, it's not a good idea to tell a woman how much money you make. This, is self explanatory. My dad taught me this. I'm not saying you should hide it, or keep a stash squirreled away in some bank account, I'm saying that you should provide for her, and allow her a sufficient amount of 'mad money', but you can be sure that if she knows of how much money you earn, she'll most likely become the ultimate consumer, and your paycheck won't even slow up when it gets to you. You will hear women say that money doesn't matter. Go ahead, move Moses off the mountain once again, because I am not buying into that. Money may not be the first thing to women, but you can bet that it's way ahead of whatever is in second place.

Never give in to her if she resorts to crying. That's emotional blackmail. They're good at it. Now if she's crying because of something you did or said, then yea, you're an asshole. Never cause a woman tears – unless you're giving her diamonds, roses or multiple orgasms.

Never cry <u>over</u> a woman. They look upon that with disgust, as if it displays emotional instability and weakness. Ok, so she hurt your feelings, but you don't have to show it to her. Besides, a woman will know when she has hurt a man.

Never fondle or otherwise touch her intimate body parts while in public. Everyone knows they're there, you don't need to point them out. You wouldn't want her grabbing you by your schnitzel and leading you around like a pull toy would you?

Never force sex on her. There are times when she just may not want any intimacy, just as there are times when you don't feel like it either. So don't push any bonding of the loins. However, a headache that lasts for 18 months is a problem – get her to a doctor.

Keep your fingernails clean and trimmed. If you're going out on a date, or if you just met her, they'll notice things like that. She won't like it if you have some foreign substance underneath your nails, especially if she's thinking about going to bed with you.

If you're feeling like you want to play 'hide the weenie', try to clean up a bit first. She isn't going to respond to your amore if you smell like a football locker room at half time. Use deodorant and a mouthwash whenever possible, or better yet, take a shower.

Never comment on her weight, unless you're both just joking around. Even then, it could strike a nerve with her, so just to play it safe, don't make any remarks about any accumulation of 'baggage'. If you feel compelled to, as a regard to her health, then you should bring it up. But if you think she's just putting on some pounds, no need to mention it. Ok, so what if when she sits in the bathtub the water level in the toilet rises, or if she sits on your face you can't hear the stereo anymore, just keep it to yourself. Besides, before you bring up any weight issue, best to check your own cargo first.

Those of you guys who have a special lady and are living together as one, give some thought to helping out with the boring, ho-hum tasks around the homestead. If you stop and think about it, if you help with the chores, then that leaves more time for - guess what - 'playtime'. So help out with the dishes, the laundry, cleaning and other phases of domestic engineering. Men as a rule, are not as emphatic about cleaning as a woman is, but it doesn't matter if you think the place is clean enough, if she says it needs to be cleaned, then help her clean it. Women can see a spec of dirt at 10 paces, whereas a man doesn't recognize dirt until there is enough to sustain enough grass growth to cover a football field. So accept her clean-routine, and you might even discover that something was in fact, dirty. You can make a game of it, and you both might find that you can have fun at the same time. Use your imagination.

The main bottom line guys, is communication, communication, communication. Relationships thrive on it. Sure, there comes the time when we all want our 'private time' by ourselves, but for solidarity, you need to have communication. Without it, your relationship isn't going anywhere except down.

Have your time with your buddy's doing 'guy things', but have some 'prime time' with your lady. Take her out.

Often. Doesn't matter if it's a planned evening, a spur-of-the-moment event or simply going out for a game of pool or having a few beers together. If it's a planned happening, or formal event, you can bet she'll take a long time getting ready for it. Accept this, for it is inevitable as the sunrise. Oddly enough, if it's a spur-of-the-moment, all she may want to do is a "P.T.A." This is a female invented acronym for simply washing her Pussy, Tits & Armpits.

Spend time with her. Even if it's just sitting out on the grass together and looking at the clouds, or taking a walk around the block, just spend time together. Laugh together. Look into each others' eyes. Sometimes the most important things and feelings are said when the eyes are doing the talking.

There's football, baseball, basketball and car races on almost every weekend, but you never know when you might miss out on a special moment by not being with your lady. As for the ladies that are reading this, do not construe this as an open invitation or some golden opportunity to expect your fella to forsake sports. Men have to have sports. It's like women and shopping. Sports & shopping - look at it as sort of a life-support system.

Never lie to a woman. There's the instinct thing again. They know. It may be some linkup with the celestial forces, but they know. Bullshitting is permitted. Most of them can see through that too, but it makes them smile.

Chapter Ten

Conclusion

What I have written is by no means the extent of women – the feminine creature that we, as men, will always pursue. It is but merely a culmination of what I feel as the most common things about women that a man should be aware of in his relating to women. It is based on what I have learned from women and observed about women. I haven't expounded with all of that which I learned, as some things are not confirmed as yet and some things are simply moot, but with each encounter with women, I find myself learning more and more. Maybe someday I'll write a volume two, I don't know. I hope this book put a smile on some faces, and but the intention is that this writing will create better relationships for men and their women alike.

As with all things in life, we have to give a little if we expect to take a little. This also applies to our relationships with women. And, it also applies to them as well. Consider it a balance between two entirely different beings dealing with everyday living. Men will always be and act as men do, women will always be and act as women do. It is up to both sexes to realize that we are each created with our own ways, and our own methods and with our own everything - no matter how weird or odd it may seem to the other gender. I think maybe The Almighty made it this way so we wouldn't get bored with each other.

As with any relationship, romance or marriage, you'll only get out what the both of you put in it. Your efforts as well as hers. It has to be worked at, nurtured and cared for. Neither of you should 'establish rules' for the other to abide by. That's controlling. Realize that the both of you are giving up 'independence' for 'inter-dependence'. Should either of you take it for granted, it will fall apart. Once this happens, it will never be the same. You can try to rebuild it, and it may become even better. But whether it gets better or whether it gets worse, there is one thing for sure - it will <u>never,</u> be the same. So take care of it! It's a give and take position, share and share alike. Nobody should have the 'upper hand', and neither of you should feel they have to drink upstream from the other. You should regard it as though the two of you are to go through life side by side. Not one in front of the other, not one behind the other, but side by side, together.

Unless there's land mines. Coin toss.